Also by Susan M. Tillery

Essentials of Personal Financial Planning,
coauthored with Thomas N. Tillery
(AICPA and Wiley, 2017)

Purses Everywhere

Susan M Tillery

PURSES EVERYWHERE

iUniverse books may be ordered through booksellers or by contacting:

iUniverse
1663 Liberty Drive
Bloomington, IN 47403
www.iuniverse.com
844-349-9409

ISBN: 978-1-6632-4282-2 (sc)
ISBN: 978-1-6632-4284-6 (hc)
ISBN: 978-1-6632-4283-9 (e)

Library of Congress Control Number: 2022913435

Print information available on the last page.

iUniverse rev. date: 09/21/2022

To all women called to a higher purpose in life. I hope this book will increase your financial understanding and confidence and lead you to financial freedom. I pray the knowledge you glean from this book will bring strength and wisdom; victory over any oppression or defeatist mentality regarding your finances; and empowerment to reach your goals, fulfill your calling, and accomplish what you were placed on this earth to do.

I've learned that you shouldn't go through life with a catcher's mitt on both hands; you need to be able to throw something back.

—Maya Angelou, interview with Oprah

She opens her arms to the poor and extends her hand to the needy.

—Proverbs 31:20 NIV

CONTENTS

As for you, be fruitful and increase in number;
multiply on the earth and increase upon it.

—Genesis 9:7 NIV

PREFACE

My education and training are in tax and personal finances. I started my career with Arthur Andersen & Company, which was one of the world's largest accounting firms before its unfortunate demise. I also worked for a national financial planning firm as well as a multi-family office and private wealth management firm. By serving individuals and families for more than thirty-five years, I have experienced just about every scenario a family may encounter with their finances. I have worked with people who have little in the way of finances and people who have more than they ever thought possible. While I spent most years implementing tax and financial plans for high-net-worth clients, I learned that regardless of the amount of wealth they have, most families have the same financial issues. The only difference is where the decimal is placed in the dollar amount they have.

No matter the degree of wealth, all families struggle with spending, budgeting, giving, saving, investing, and filing taxes. However, I have observed that high-net-worth families struggle more, mainly due to the responsibility that accompanies their large amount of wealth. These families have much more to be accountable for, and they are in the position of attracting unscrupulous individuals who desire to take from them. A high-net-worth individual or family is sued, ripped off, and stolen from more often than the rest of us are. They pay much more in taxes as a percentage of income, yet of all the families I have had the privilege to work with, the high-net-worth families recognize their need for help to a much greater degree than the rest of us. It is wise to seek expert advice and counsel in areas where we do not have the required expertise, knowledge, or understanding. Those who do not ask for help suffer unnecessarily. They may feel they have enough knowledge to get by; or they may feel they are supposed to have this knowledge, and pride keeps them from seeking counsel. Asking for and seeking help is step number one. By picking up this book, you are seeking counsel and have already begun your journey to financial freedom.

Those who desire to be good stewards of their resources ask for help, and as a result, they attain wisdom, knowledge, and understanding. Financial stewardship is accomplished by creating and keeping to a spending plan; reducing taxes through appropriate tax-planning measures; properly using debt; investing wisely; giving; and multiplying what one has, instead of clutching it or hiding it due to fear. It's not the amount of money a person has that matters but, rather, how it is managed.

> As for you, be fruitful and increase in number; multiply on the earth and increase upon it. (Genesis 9:7 NIV)

I decided to write this book to help those who desire wisdom, knowledge, and understanding but are not able to afford or find someone to help them manage their finances. I was a single mom for seven years, so my heart's desire is to help women gain this knowledge and understanding in order to attain financial peace of mind and security for themselves and their families and to be effective stewards of all they have. I hope once they're empowered, they will, in turn, help and empower others.

One of my dreams is for all women and children to be free and have the opportunity to reach their goals and follow their God-given callings in life. In a country that believes in life, liberty, and the pursuit of happiness, one would think this would be an easy dream to see fulfilled. Unfortunately, it is not. There is no one reason why this is the case. However, I believe one way this can change is to educate women about personal finances, which will give them full purses without holes through which their finances disappear.

Then these women, with the knowledge and empowerment they experience through financial security, will turn to help other women and children who cannot help themselves, especially those who are not free and those who are in poverty.

There are many women and children in the United States who are in bondage, held against their will, and trafficked as slaves. There are also millions of women and children in this country who are in bondage due to poverty. According to the US Institute Against Human Trafficking, there are nearly 40.3 million victims of human and sex trafficking worldwide, with 75 percent of them being women and girls and 25 percent being children. The institute believes the number of children trafficked in the United States is by far in excess of one hundred thousand.[1] Additionally, one in nine women (or 13.9 million) and one in seven children (nearly 10.5 million) lived in poverty in the United States in 2019.[2] The scriptures say we are to do the following:

> Rescue those being led away to death; hold back those staggering toward slaughter. If you say, "But we knew nothing about this," does not He who weighs the heart perceive it? Does not He who guards your life know it? Will he not repay everyone according to what they have done? (Proverbs 24:11–12 NIV)

When we, as women, become empowered through the financial principles in this book and, as a result, are able to help ourselves and our families, imagine what will happen when we all come together and bring our resources—which I refer to as *full purses* throughout this book—to help those who are held in bondage, whether through trafficking or through poverty. By our coming together to bring freedom to these women and children, may future generations say, regarding our generation, "They rescued those being led away to death, and purses were everywhere because women

---

[1] U.S. Institute Against Human Trafficking, http://usiaht.org/the-problem/#facts-about-human-trafficking.

[2] Amanda Finn, "National Snapshot: Poverty among Women and Families, 2020," National Women's Law Center, December 2020, https://nwlc.org/wp-content/uploads/2020/12/PovertySnapshot2020.pdf.

stood together and combined their purses [resources] to help."

For this to happen, we all must have our individual financial houses in order first. We will then have the purses (resources), wisdom, knowledge, and understanding necessary to tackle this evil and injustice.

Thank you for believing and trusting in yourself enough to read and apply the principles in this book. You are on your way to a new journey of empowering yourself and your family. The knowledge you gain will deepen your understanding and bring you financial security and financial order. This book will position you to utilize this knowledge and strength for ultimate good, and you will be able to empower other women and children who are not able to help themselves.

The profits generated from the sale of this book will be donated to help women and children living in poverty or trapped in trafficking or abuse. Thank you for being part of this generation who will bring down economic injustice in our country and world.

I would like to thank Jacquie Tyre for her spiritual insights, as well as her recommendations and encouragement. I would like to thank Angela Ramage for her assistance and encouragement at the early stages when the idea of this book first began to take shape. I would also like to thank my husband, Tom, for his contribution and love. He is the greatest financial planner I know. I have learned so much from him.

You do not have because you do not ask God. When you ask, you do not receive, because you ask with wrong motives, that you may spend what you get on your pleasures.

—James 4:2–3 NIV

INTRODUCTION

THERE ARE SEVEN BASIC FINANCIAL PRINCIPLES THAT BRING financial order and peace to whoever chooses to apply them, regardless of the amount of net worth one has. These principles are laid out in this short book, *Purses Everywhere*. I intentionally wrote the book to be brief so it would not be a burden to read. We live in such a fast-paced world that we barely take time to breathe deeply anymore, let alone set aside time to read a financial book. Most people would rather run to keep up with the disorder and chaos in their financial lives than take the time to read a book and gain the wisdom they need to bring peace into their financial lives.

Purses Everywhere focuses on helping you set goals to implement these seven financial principles in your life. Most of us are not looking to be rich; we just want to have peace in our financial lives and enough to provide for our families and be able to help others. We are made with an inherent desire to help others. But before we can do this, we must help ourselves first. Just as airline attendants share before any flight takes off, you must put your own oxygen mask on first and then put one on your child. In order to really help someone, you must first help yourself.

The book begins with a short historical story about the origin of purses in order to emphasize the connection between our purses, or resources, and our financial health. I use this analogy throughout the book. If our purses are full, we can join together with other women whose purses are full to free women and children who are not able to help themselves. I believe there will be a moment in time when purses are everywhere!

The seven principles I will discuss are giving, the Rule of 72, financial ratios, spending plans, emergency reserves and savings, investing, and thankfulness. They are a mixture of basic financial planning principles and biblical principles. You don't have to be a Christian to garner truth and freedom from this book. Don't let my faith get in the way of your financial freedom; you may ignore the scripture references, but don't ignore the principles. I have written this book to help all women bring financial order and peace to their lives with the belief they will help others do the same by passing this book along to them; giving to or loving them; and, ultimately, freeing them from whatever bondage they are in.

As I mentioned earlier, I was a single mom for seven years. If not for the Lord and my parents, I would not have survived financially. Once I got back on my feet after my divorce, the Lord taught me about His principles of stewardship through Crown Ministries, a twelve-week course in which I learned we were designed to ask for help. The Bible says we have not because we ask not: "You do not have because you do not ask God. When you ask, you do not receive, because you ask with wrong motives, that you may spend what you get on your pleasures" (James 4:2 – 3 NIV).

Through the Crown course, I learned to set goals, prioritize them, and share them with others. I never before had seen, and have not seen since, such financial miracles occur as when we prayed for one another. Humans were not designed to be self-sufficient; we were made to help one another, asking for help when we need it and giving help when it is in our power to do so. This keeps us from becoming prideful and creates a sense of community among us.

Writing this book is my way of helping all who are suffering and are grappling with how to change their circumstances. This book is also my way of helping young people in high school or college start their financial lives on the right foot and not have to experience the pain and suffering that accompanies ignorance of financial principles.

Let's begin this journey with a little bit of history about purses and a discussion of how they are a symbol of our financial life and why setting goals is essential in moving forward. We will discuss what creates holes in our purses. Those holes keep us from financial peace and order in our lives, which in turn keeps us from being able to help others and experience the joy that accompanies helping those in need. This journey will take time, but anything worth having is worth working for and persevering in prayer for. I believe you picked up this book because you want your purse to be full in order to bless your family and others.

You have planted much, but have harvested little. You eat, but never have enough. You drink, but never have your fill. You put on clothes, but are not warm. You earn wages, only to put them in a purse with holes in it.

—Haggai 1:6 NIV

CHAPTER 1
PURSES AND GOALS

Purses

MOST WOMEN CARRY A PURSE. SOME PURSES ARE LARGE, AND some are small, but nearly every woman carries a purse. A purse carries our money, and for some women, it becomes a small suitcase holding any item that might be needed during the day. If a woman is married or has children, she also carries items in her purse that her family might need during the day. In case you are wondering how this practice began, I'd like to share a little history that I found interesting. It is also relevant to our topic of managing money.

Throughout history, handbags have served both men and women as tools for mobility. While we commonly think of handbags as primarily for women, history shows that handbags have been used by both genders for thousands of years. This has quite a bit to do with the fact that men's clothing had no pockets until the seventeenth century.[3]

During the time when pockets did not exist in clothing, small purses or bags were utilized for a variety of reasons. I found one of these reasons especially interesting: a small bag called an *almoner*, which got its name from the Christian principle of almsgiving, was used to carry coins to give to the poor.

Women were especially attracted to ornate drawstring purses. For the wealthy, bags were used as gifts and gestures of courtship and were often carefully decorated with romantic scenes. On the other hand, laborers used simplistic bags to carry tools and necessities during their work.

Even the Bible mentions purses in scripture. The following verse begins our journey about managing our money:

> You have planted much, but have harvested little. You eat, but never have enough. You drink, but never have your fill. You put on clothes, but are not warm. You earn wages, only to put them in a purse with holes in it. (Haggai 1:6 NIV)

Do you ever find yourself saying, "I work so hard but have nothing left at the end of the month. It's as if my money

---

[3] 5-Minute History, 2016, https://fiveminutehistory.com/the-history-of-handbags-a-5-minute-guide/.

just disappears. I want to help others, but I can't even help myself or my family"? The financial principles in this book will bring you new understanding and help you set goals that will enable you to have a full purse without holes.

It's unfortunate that our schools and even our colleges don't teach the basics of managing money. I find it odd that I was taught subjects in school that, while interesting and even fascinating, were not that important. The knowledge of managing money wisely, which is critical for all of us to understand, was not taught. The number-one subject that could make our lives easier and more manageable, keep marriages together, and even be fun is not taught in most schools. Instead, we either have to learn it the hard way or don't learn it at all. By following the principles in this book and setting goals, you will gain knowledge and understanding that will bring financial wisdom to your life.

Setting Goals

This short book lays out basic money-management principles that will help bring order to your financial life. It is a short book because time is limited, especially if you are married or have children or a demanding career. If you will take just a little time out for yourself to read the following pages, you will garner the basic principles of financial freedom and be equipped to develop some excellent financial goals for yourself and your family.

Speaking of goals, Brian Tracy, a great motivational speaker, said, "People with clear, written goals, accomplish far more in a shorter period of time than people without them could ever imagine." A goal written down is more likely to be accomplished than one that is not. Additionally, if you share your goals with someone else and make yourself accountable to that person, your chance of reaching your goals is even higher.

According to a study done by Dr. Gail Matthews at Dominican University,[4] 76 percent of individuals who wrote down their goals, shared them with a friend, and then sent a weekly progress report to that friend accomplished their goals. Compare this to those who had goals in mind but never committed the goals to writing: only 43 percent of this group accomplished their goals.

In the introduction, I mentioned I completed the Crown financial course. During that time, I committed my financial goals to writing for the first time. I had an accountability partner, and we prayed together about each other's goals weekly. At the time I was taking the class, my son and I were living with my parents, so my first goal was to find a new job that paid well enough to permit me to move into an apartment and reestablish financial order in my life.

As a result of writing down my goal, establishing accountability to another person, and being faithful to pray, I attained my goal. I would like to add that no one knocked on my door to ask me to come to work for them; rather, I prayed about the goal and obeyed whatever the Lord put on my heart to do. As a result, I received a position with a great company that was beyond my wildest

---

[4] Gail Matthews, Dominican University of California, 2015, https://scholar. dominican.edu/cgi/viewcontent.cgi?article=1265&context=news-releases.

expectations. Needless to say, I was thankful. That was one of many written goals I achieved. Through my new job, the Lord restored much of what I had lost before the divorce. Additionally, the financial course changed my thinking and mindset. I learned and understood what my responsibilities are and what God's responsibilities are; this is the key.

An important note about goals: our goals line up with our thinking, and our thinking lines up with our understanding. I hope that by investing a small amount of time to read this book, you will gain a new understanding of money-management principles, which will then offer you the opportunity to change how you think about money and, as a result, enable you to set goals that will lead to your financial freedom.

Imagine what could happen if women all over the country understood the financial principles I'm going to share with you. Not only would they gain financial freedom for themselves and their families, but they also could help others. Financially free individuals and families with resources available to share with the less fortunate could even join their purses with churches, communities, and charitable organizations. The nation would then have the vision for eradicating poverty.

This movement, due to the sheer number of financially free individuals and families, could then help women globally to attain this understanding and financial freedom. Resources would become available to rescue women trapped in poverty and trafficking around the world.

I believe women are called to help one another, not hate one another due to different political or religious beliefs.

Deep down inside, each one of us desires to help everyone have freedom, whether it's financial freedom or freedom from slavery and indignity.

Action Step

Grab a pen and paper; and as you read the financial principles in each chapter, write down your goals, and begin eliminating any holes in your purse immediately. Then share your goals with a friend, and send your friend a weekly progress report. This book is about keeping it simple. My mother called it the KISS method: keep it simple, sweetie.

A stingy sower will reap a meager harvest, but the one who sows from a generous spirit will reap an abundant harvest. Let giving flow from your heart, not from a sense of religious duty. Let it spring up freely from the joy of giving—all because God loves hilarious generosity.

—2 Corinthians 9:6–7 TPT

One person gives freely, yet gains even more; another withholds unduly, but comes to poverty. A generous person will prosper; whoever refreshes others will be refreshed.

—Proverbs 11:24–25 NIV

Give and it will be given to you. A good measure, pressed down, shaken together and running over, will be poured into your lap. For with the measure you use, it will be measured to you.

—Luke 6:38 NIV

CHAPTER 2
GIVING

I WILL BEGIN THIS DISCUSSION OF THE JOURNEY TO FINANCIAL freedom not by talking about how to accumulate more wealth but by sharing how important it is to give. If you are struggling with money, then giving may seem like the craziest idea you have ever heard. But giving is something special that brings great joy, and it is also something that God created us to do. Psychologists have proven that when we give, we are happier. It's also one of the ways we can monitor greed, selfishness, and fear in ourselves.

Fear is something we all deal with. Jerome and Patti were no exception, and their story tells us what fear can do when it gets out of control. They were in their eighties, and just before her eighty-first birthday, Patti passed away. Jerome asked our firm to help him with probate court and the distribution of money to Patti's children according to her will (it was the second marriage for both Jerome and

Patti). First, we went through boxes of records, receipts, and statements and compiled a net-worth statement so we could see what Jerome and Patti's assets and liabilities were and which assets were titled in Patti's name, so the correct assets were distributed. Then we sat down with Jerome and shared with him what his net-worth statement showed and which assets (e.g., cash, stocks, house, car) needed to be distributed to Patti's children. Jerome wept and was shocked when we divulged his net worth. It was ten times more than the amount he'd thought it was. He started shaking, and one of the first things he said was that he and Patti had stopped giving to their church and other charities because they had been afraid they were going to run out of money.

Listening to the news and enduring more than a year of COVID-19 fear had stopped Patti and Jerome from doing something they enjoyed: giving. After distributing the assets to Patti's children and grandchildren per the instructions in the will, Jerome made it a priority to start giving again, and his joy was reestablished. Certainly, he is still grieving Patti's death, but he knows she is smiling down on him because the fear is gone.

This fear was irrational and increased as time went on. Irrational decisions were made that stole Jerome and Patti's joy, their peace of mind, and one of their most important shared values: giving. If you have stopped giving, you may want to consider if fear is at the root of this decision. If you've never been a giver, ask yourself why. Giving or not giving can reveal a lot about us.

One person gives freely, yet gains even
more; another withholds unduly, but comes
to poverty. A generous person will prosper;
whoever refreshes others will be refreshed.
(Proverbs 11:24–25 NIV)

When we give, we display love for our fellow man and
place others' needs in front of our own. This brings great
joy, no matter how much we give. When we give, we are
actually planting a seed. As with all seeds, the seed we plant
will grow and give back much more. If you are skeptical
of this, then practice this principle by giving something. It
may be to a church; a charitable organization; or perhaps a
family member, a friend, or even someone you do not know.
Give what you feel comfortable giving, no matter how little
or how much.

Then watch what happens to you inside. Also watch
what happens down the road as your giving seed grows.
You will be amazed; when you least expect it, or when
you need it most, someone will give to you. It may be a
family member, an employer through a raise, or a complete
stranger. Be alert, though, because you may not recognize
it when it comes back to you! But be sure of this: you reap
what you sow.

A stingy sower will reap a meager harvest,
but the one who sows from a generous spirit
will reap an abundant harvest. Let giving
flow from your heart, not from a sense of
religious duty. Let it spring up freely from the

joy of giving—all because God loves hilarious generosity. (2 Corinthians 9:6–7 TPT)

If you are Jewish or Christian, you most likely have been taught about tithing. *Tithe* means "a tenth," and if you have been giving 10 percent to your church or temple, you have already experienced the joy and provision that accompany giving. If you are not able or don't have the desire to give 10 percent, how about 1 percent? It is important to start somewhere.

If you feel you don't have the resources to give anything, then you may want to think about giving your time. Giving time to an organization or an individual is another form of giving. Great things happen when you give your time to someone else. A marriage can be refreshed, a child can blossom, an addict can feel hope again, or a lonely person can feel loved.

We all have so much to give, whether it is money, time, love, services, or possessions. The list is endless. Try giving. Then watch joy come into your heart, and see how your needs are taken care of!

> Give, and it will be given to you. A good measure, pressed down, shaken together, and running over, will be poured into your lap. For with the measure you use, it will be measured to you. (Luke 6:38 NIV)

God loves a cheerful giver. There is no greater way to eliminate holes in our purses than by giving. Everyone would agree that it makes sense to eliminate the holes in our purses before we fill them up. That's why this book begins with giving; it's the one sure way to eliminate the holes. With this new understanding, let's move on to the first step we need to take in order to start filling our purses.

Suggested Goals

Speak out loud to yourself the following affirmation daily: "I am a cheerful giver!"

Set your goal for giving, whether it be money, time, love, services, or possessions, to a charity, church, elderly parent, grandparent, neighbor, or other person.

_____% of my gross pay (the amount before taxes and 401(k) contributions)

or

_____% of my net pay (the amount that actually is deposited into your bank account)

or

$_____ per day, $___ per week, or $___ per month

or

my time, love, services, or possessions

to _____ (church, nonprofit organization, person)

There is no right or wrong way to begin giving. What's important is that you begin and set a goal to give.

My people are destroyed from lack of knowledge.

—Hosea 4:6 NIV

CHAPTER 3

THE RULE OF 72

I RECALL DRIVING THROUGH A BEAUTIFUL ATLANTA SUBURB one summer afternoon and seeing all the lovely, grand homes. I stopped, closed my eyes, and said, "Heavenly Father, why do some people have and some don't?"

The answer surprised me. "Daughter," He said, "those who have understand the principles of wealth, especially how to make money work for them, including the Rule of 72."

Now, there are many reasons why some have wealth and some don't. But I believe the Lord gave me this particular insight that summer day because He was asking me to do something about the lack of knowledge that most of us have regarding money. As a CPA financial planner, I understand financial principles and the Rule of 72, and I am able to share this knowledge with clients, friends, family, and anyone who asks about money. This was the genesis of my writing this book.

On that same day, I also reflected on the fact that even though I had been a CPA for many years and had a master's degree in accounting, I had not learned about the Rule of 72 in college. It wasn't until I attended a conference fifteen years after graduating that I learned the Rule of 72. I decided at that moment to share this aspect of money with everyone who would listen.

Simply stated, the Rule of 72 says that when you divide the number 72 by the rate of return you are earning on your money, you will know how soon your money will double. Yes, by doing nothing other than leaving your money in a retirement account earning a rate of return, such as an IRA, Roth IRA, 401(k), or other investment account, your money will double over time.

Let's look at an example of how the Rule of 72 works. If Stephanie, age twenty-two, puts $6,000 in an investment account and earns an average of 6 percent on her money, the Rule of 72 says her money will double in twelve years without her adding any additional money to the account. (Divide 72 by her interest rate of 6 percent: 72 / 6 = 12.) In twelve years, Stephanie will have $12,000 if all she does is put in $6,000. In another twelve years, she will have $24,000, and in another twelve years, her original $6,000 investment will be $48,000.

If, instead, Stephanie places $6,000 in her investment account every year, each $6,000 doubles every twelve years, and by the time she retires in forty years, Stephanie will have accumulated $928,572!

What if Stephanie was to earn 8 percent on her money instead of 6 percent? This would mean her money will double every nine years (72 / 8 = 9), and her $6,000-a-year investment will accumulate to $1,554,339 in forty years. This is not too shabby, considering she only put away $500 per month ($6,000 per year).

Note: The Rule of 72 does not take into account any fees charged by an investment manager, so the numbers are approximate rather than exact. This does suggest, however, that it is worth taking the time to negotiate fees if possible. However, the fact that Stephanie's money is doubling (working for her) without her doing anything is the point being made here. Just think what will happen if Stephanie sticks to her plan and does not withdraw her money until retirement.

Imagine your money working for you, instead of you working for it! This is a completely different perspective. This is an example of new understanding, which then brings new thinking, which brings new goals and financial freedom. Wealthy people understand this principle, and it greatly affects their goals and outcomes. But many others have never heard about this formula for financial success. I believe this lack of knowledge is a main contributor to the difference in economic levels in our country.

> My people are destroyed from lack of knowledge. (Hosea 4:6 NIV)

This is the miracle of compound interest. Einstein said, "It is the greatest discovery ever!" The second principle of gaining financial freedom and having a full purse is understanding and applying this miracle of compound interest in your life by putting your money to work for you.

It is mind-boggling to think about why this concept is not taught in schools. Money concepts should begin in grade school and continue through college. The fact that so many of us are not aware of the greatest discovery ever speaks to why so many do not prosper in a country as prosperous as the United States.

It's plain and simple. You can have your money work for you and change your life by having financial freedom. Or you can spend your life working for money and watching it slip right out of the holes in your purse. It is not about how much you make but about how you manage what you have: how much you spend, how much you save, and how much of your money is working for you by your benefitting from the Rule of 72.

I believe if you teach your children the Rule of 72 as well as the other principles in this book, you will change your family's future by leaving them this legacy. Generations of families can have purses without holes and can be part of the Purses Everywhere movement.

As I shared in chapter 1, we must be willing to gain new understanding before our thinking will change, and our new thinking will lead us to the goals that will empower us to attain financial freedom. You now understand how important the Rule of 72 is and why it is so important to invest and have money working for you. The next five chapters will give you the opportunity to change your thinking about financial principles, which will enable you to set goals that will lead you to financial freedom and a full purse with no holes.

Let's move on to our next chapter on financial ratios. Chapter 4 will help you learn how to have money available in your current situation so you can begin to invest and let your money work for you.

Suggested Goals

Speak out loud to yourself daily the following affirmation:

> I manage my money well and use the Rule of 72 to make money work for me. As soon as it is available to me, following the financial principles in this book, I will put money in an investment account that grows.

The rich rule over the poor, and the
borrower is slave to the lender.

—Proverbs 22:7 NIV

If any of you lacks wisdom, you should ask God, who
gives generously to all without finding fault, and it will
be given to you. But when you ask, you must believe
and not doubt, because the one who doubts is like
a wave of the sea, blown and tossed by the wind.

—James 1:5–6 NIV

CHAPTER 4
DEBT-MANAGEMENT RATIOS

FINANCIAL RATIOS ARE A KEY COMPONENT IN THE JOURNEY TO financial freedom. These ratios provide well-established guidelines used by CPAs and other financial professionals to determine appropriate spending and borrowing guidelines. Before you crinkle up your nose and perhaps stomp your foot and say to yourself, "No, I can't [or don't want to] change my spending habits," remember, we are looking for ways to free up money to invest so the Rule of 72 works for you and, as a result, your purse begins to fill up. Therefore, it is necessary to look at how you currently use the money you receive.

There are three established debt-management ratios. If individuals or families adapt their spending to fall within these ratios, they are on the path to having monies available to invest, thereby opening the door for the Rule of 72 to work for them. This, in turn, will fill their purses and lead them on the journey to financial freedom.

> The rich rule over the poor and the borrower
> is slave to the lender. (Proverbs 22:7 NIV)

The first ratio is called the Housing Expense ratio. An individual's Housing Expense ratio should be less than 28 percent of their gross income. Gross income is all income before taxes and deductions. (Net income is the income remaining after deductions and taxes, or said another way, it is what you actually deposit into your bank account from each paycheck.) If you own a home, your mortgage payment, property taxes, and homeowner's insurance (referred to as PITI) should be less than 28 percent of your gross income in order for you to remain, or put yourself, on the path to financial freedom.

Let's look at an example: Gina makes $50,000 per year at her job. She has no other income, so $50,000 is her gross income. Twenty-eight percent of $50,000 is $14,000. Therefore, her rent and renter's insurance or mortgage payment (*principal* and *interest*), property *taxes*, and homeowner's *insurance* (PITI) should be less than $14,000 per year, or $1,167 ($14,000 / 12) per month. Always keep the Housing Expense ratio in mind whenever you are considering the purchase of a home or the rental of a house or apartment. If you stay within this guideline, you will not create a hole in your purse.

If you are in a house or apartment and realize you are not within the guidelines, consider moving if it's an option. Many times, it is not an option; if this is the case, pay special attention to the other two debt ratios.

Clients Elizabeth and John provided a stunning example of what can happen when you don't pay attention to your financial ratios. Elizabeth and John are quite wealthy; they have wealth that most advisers would label as *high net worth*. However, recently, they were turned down for an automobile loan. They were shocked and perplexed. The bank told them their Total Monthly Debt ratio (the next ratio I will discuss) was too high. Elizabeth and John, both entrepreneurs, put all their business expenses on a credit card, and most of the time, they went over the card limit. But they paid off their entire credit card bill each month, and the credit card company never said anything to them, nor were they penalized or charged any interest. However, unbeknownst to them, the credit card company reported to the credit reporting agencies that they went over their limit each month. This brought their credit score of 850 down to 600. This occurred even though Elizabeth and John paid off their total credit card balances every month. Our firm strongly encourages all our clients to check their credit reports three times a year; however, Elizabeth and John had not done so. When they called us to tell us they were turned down for a loan, we immediately sent them to check their credit report. When they did, they found notations stating that they were consistently over their debt limit for a particular credit card. They contacted the credit card company and asked for and were given a higher credit limit since they paid the card off each month. Hopefully, they will not have this type of horrible surprise again.

The second debt ratio, referred to as the Total Monthly Debt ratio, is the ratio Elizabeth and John took their eye off. This ratio measures all of an individual's debt payments. The guidelines state this ratio should be less than 36 percent of gross income. This includes mortgage payments, car payments, credit card payments, student loan payments, and personal loan payments. If we look back at Gina's information in our first example, in order for Gina to be within the guidelines, her total debt payments need to be less than $20,160 per year ($50,000 gross income × 36 percent), or $1,680 per month (20,160 / 12).

The third debt ratio is the Consumer Debt ratio, which measures consumer debt payments. This ratio should be less than 20 percent of an individual's net income. In our example, Gina's gross income is $50,000, but her net income, or take-home pay, for the year is $38,000 after taxes. Therefore, to be in line with this ratio, her consumer debt payments should not exceed $7,600 ($38,000 × 20 percent) per year, or $633 (7,600 / 12) per month. This includes car loans and credit cards.

Let's review the debt-management ratios one more time:

1. Housing expenses (principal, interest, taxes, and homeowner's insurance or rent and renter's insurance) need to be less than 28 percent of gross income.

2. Total monthly debt needs to be less than 36 percent of gross income.
3. Consumer debt needs to be less than 20 percent of net income.

Once you have your financial ratios equal to or less than these guidelines, you are well on your way to eliminating the holes in your purse and will have enough to save and invest in order for the Rule of 72 to work for you. If one or more of your ratios exceeds the guidelines, you have your next goal: (1) reduce your debt or housing costs or (2) increase your income. These are major decisions and need to be prayerfully considered.

> If any of you lacks wisdom, you should ask God, who gives generously to all without finding fault, and it will be given to you. But when you ask, you must believe and not doubt, because the one who doubts is like a wave of the sea, blown and tossed by the wind. (James 1:5–6 NIV)

Ask God for guidance, wisdom, and understanding, and persevere in prayer. Recall my prayer when I asked for a job that would provide well enough to permit me to move into an apartment and reestablish financial order in my life. The Lord answered that prayer, but I had to ask. One of the names for God is Jehovah-Jireh, the God who provides. He may show you a way to make extra income or even start a business in order to pay off a debt, provide you with a strategy to reduce expenses, or provide for a raise. This could take some time, but Jehovah-Jireh will not let you down.

Suggested Goals

1. First calculate your monthly income amounts to be used in the calculation of your debt-management ratios below.

    Gross income $_____ × 28% = _____ / 12 _____

    Gross income $_____ × 36% = _____ / 12 _____

    Net income $_____ × 20% = _____ / 12 _____

2. Then calculate all three of your monthly debt-management ratios:

    A. Housing Expense ratio: < 28% of gross income

        Mortgage payment (principal and interest) _____

        Property taxes _____

        Homeowner's insurance _____

        Total _____

or

Rent _____

Renter's insurance_____

Total _____

Is your total less than 28 percent of your gross income? If yes, you are heading in the right direction. If no, you may want to make an adjustment.

B. Total Monthly Debt ratio: < 36% of gross income

Mortgage _____

Credit cards _____

School loans _____

Car payments _____

Other _____

Total _____

Are your total payments less than 36 percent of your gross income? If yes, you are heading in the right direction. If no, you may want to make an adjustment.

C. Consumer Debt ratio: < 20% of net income

Credit cards _____

Car loans _____

Total _____

Are your total payments less than 20 percent of your net income? If yes, you are heading in the right direction. If no, you may want to make an adjustment.

3. If any of your debt-management ratios are too high, write a goal to reduce expenses or increase income. This may take some time and diligence, but persevere. The rewards will be great.

I will reduce expenses by $_____ and/or increase earnings by $_____ to pay off my debt in _____ months or years.

The reduction in expenses will occur by _____.

I will increase income by _____.

Brilliant ideas pay off and bring you prosperity, but making hasty, impatient decisions will only lead to financial loss.

—Proverbs 21:5 TPT

CHAPTER 5
SPENDING PLAN

Do you hate the word *budget*? Me too! It can conjure up thoughts of constraints, lack of freedom and spontaneity, and other negative connotations. This is why I have changed the name of this tool to a spending plan, which describes exactly what it is: a plan for spending. If you fail to have a plan, as the saying goes, then you plan to fail. You will find spending spiraling out of control and holes opening up in your purse at an alarming rate.

> Brilliant ideas pay off and bring you prosperity, but making hasty, impatient decisions will only lead to financial loss. (Proverbs 21:5 TPT)

Pull out a piece of paper, or go online and find a spending plan (budget) template. I have my clients go to the following link: https://www.vertex42.com/ExcelTemplates/personal-budget-spreadsheet.html. Scroll down until you see "Personal Budget Spreadsheet." Click on this link to download the Excel spreadsheet. These are free spreadsheets you may download, but feel free to use whatever works for you.

Sit down, and put together your spending plan. If you are married or your budget involves another person, work together on your spending plan if possible.

First, record on the spreadsheet the monthly amount of cash coming into your bank account. List the amount you receive from your paycheck and any other cash or checks you obtain during the month. Don't forget to list child support, alimony, interest, dividends, pension, Social Security, and so on.

Second, list on the spreadsheet all the cash going out of your bank account each month for bills and spending: mortgage, rent, electricity and/or gas, water, internet, cell phone, groceries, eating out, vacation, clothing, haircuts, entertainment, hobbies, babysitting, childcare, and any other expenses you incur. For utility bills, groceries, and any other bill that varies each month (these are called variable expenses), list the actual amount from the prior year or an average amount based on the prior year or an estimate for this year. To get an accurate number, go through your check register or your online bank account, total the last twelve months in each variable spending category, and divide that number by twelve. (If twelve months is too overwhelming, then do this for at least six months.) This becomes your average expense for your variable spending categories.

This is an important exercise for all of us. As I said earlier, it is not the amount of money that matters but how it is managed or, said another way, how well we steward it. *Steward*, in this instance, means "manage." Since we are stewards of all we have, how can we be sure we steward well? The first step is to know what's coming in and what's going out.

Joseph and Celia are clients of our firm. Celia is an executive at a public company and earns a large salary. Joseph is retired and volunteers in the community. Joseph and Celia were referred to us because even though they have a large amount of income coming in every month, they have a larger amount going out. This is not sustainable. We went to work right away and created their spending plan. Once they saw how much money was going out, they immediately started cutting back. Celia was close to retirement and knew if they didn't do something quickly, they would be in a messy situation once her salary stopped coming in.

Fortunately, Celia was flexible with her retirement date, because as it turned out, they needed three years to cut back their lifestyle and pay off their credit cards. The first year, they cut back on spending in order to pay off their credit cards. During the second year, while still in credit card debt, they made additional reductions in their spending. By the third year, their credit cards were paid off, they had reduced spending, and they were putting any excess income into their investment account. Again, it's not how much you have; it's how you manage or steward it.

Now that you have created a monthly or annual spending plan, you are able to determine if you are overspending and, if so, where the hole is. If your expenses exceed your income, your next goal is to reduce your spending or increase your income by getting a second job or starting a small business on the side.

Some bills, such as your mortgage, cannot change. But expenses for eating out, clothing, entertainment, vacation, newspapers, magazines, hobbies, and so on can be reduced or eliminated while you work on reducing your spending. Once you have a spending plan in place that eliminates overspending (most likely from using credit cards), you are ready to move on to the next step.

Even if gaining control of your spending plan takes a year or longer (again, it took Joseph and Celia three years), do not be stressed. This is the most important action you can take on your road to financial freedom: spend less than you make. If you have to move and it is reasonable to do so, then begin looking for a new home or apartment. If you need to add a second job or start a business on the side, do so. What are your talents and skills? Can you tutor kids in your neighborhood, babysit, run errands for others, make things, bake, cook, drive people in your vehicle (privately or through Uber or Lyft), or work on the weekends at the local mall or grocery store? Have fun with this. Get creative, use your God-given talents and gifts, and do something you enjoy. We all have special gifts, talents, and skills given to us by God. If you enjoy something, it's probably because you are good at it. Use that talent to provide your extra income.

I want to challenge you with your next goal. Determine to have a spending plan that is equal to 50 percent (or less) of your gross income. You may think this sounds impossible, but it is the quickest way to travel down the road to financial freedom and to have a full purse with no holes.

The Tax Foundation, the nation's leading independent tax-policy nonprofit organization, published an article in May 2020 stating the average American's tax burden for federal, state and local, Social Security, and Medicare tax is 29.8 percent. This leaves 70 percent of your gross income for your bills and other needs and desires. This does not include consumption-based taxes paid, such as sales tax, property tax, or other taxes on specific items.

Add to this number your goal from chapter 2 for giving, which may be to eventually give 10 percent of your gross earnings. You now have 60 percent of your gross paycheck left. Additionally, as I will discuss in the next chapter, a suggested goal for investing (so you can have your money work for you) is 10 percent. This leaves approximately 50 percent of your gross pay available for your spending plan. Therefore, living off 50 percent of your gross income is a recommended guideline. Let this be one of your goals, and when you reach it, you will be well on your way to financial freedom. Remember, it is not how much you make; it is how you manage or steward what you have.

Suggested Goals

1. Create a spending plan for living on 50 percent of your gross pay, and work toward this goal. You can plan this out by using the template at https://www.vertex42.com/ExcelTemplates/personal-budget-spreadsheet.html. Scroll down until you see "Personal Budget Spreadsheet." Click on this link to download the Excel spreadsheet.

    Of the remaining 50 percent of your gross pay, approximately 30 percent goes to taxes.

2. This leaves 20 percent to allocate in the following manner:

    _____% for giving according to my chapter 2 goal (if giving was a monetary amount versus time, services, or possessions)

    _____% for debt reduction for my chapter 4 goal

3. If you have debt, complete the worksheet by visiting https://www.vertex42.com/Calculators/debt-reduction-calculator.html. Scroll down until you see "Debt Reduction Calculator." Click on this link, scroll down, and download the Excel spreadsheet.

The wise store up choice food and olive oil, but fools gulp theirs down.

—Proverbs 21:20 NIV

CHAPTER 6

EMERGENCY RESERVE AND SAVINGS

ONCE YOU DETERMINE AN APPROPRIATE SPENDING PLAN AND are within the debt-ratio guidelines, you are ready to move to the next step of establishing your savings.

> The wise store up choice food and olive oil,
> but fools gulp theirs down.
> (Proverbs 21:20 NIV)

There are two types of savings you will want to plan for. The first is your emergency reserve account. Your emergency reserve should contain enough money to pay for three to six months of your nondiscretionary bills.

Nondiscretionary bills are your have-to bills. You have to pay them, whether you have a job or not, such as a mortgage, utilities, insurance, minimums on credit cards, and other debt payments.

Discretionary bills are those you don't have to pay if you lose your job, such as clothing, eating out, entertainment, vacation, payments above the minimum on your credit card, babysitting, and so on. If you are married and both you and your spouse work, a three-month emergency reserve is usually sufficient. If you are single or if you are married and only one spouse works, you will need a six-month emergency reserve account.

An emergency reserve account keeps you from going into debt if you or your spouse loses a job or if a major house or car repair crops up. These things are going to happen—that's just part of life. However, if you have an appropriate emergency reserve available to handle the expected unexpected events, your purse will escape the large holes that emergencies create. These emergencies, when not planned for, tend to send us back to the beginning of our journey to financial freedom. They force us to start at step one all over again.

Joyce experienced this firsthand when her basement became mold-ridden. She called the mold mitigators, and they came to make an assessment. Her crawl space (Joyce lives in the South) had been harboring mold for years, but she'd had no idea. Joyce did not have the money for repairs; she had never even heard of an emergency fund. Joyce was not able to afford the repair, and she was frantic because she knew the mold would affect her and her daughter's health. She spent hours on the phone, obtaining additional quotes and alternatives. The lowest estimate was $12,000.

Joyce was living paycheck to paycheck and could not come up with the money for the repair. She was forced to sell her home. It was actually the best alternative for Joyce, because she had not been keeping up the home, nor had she made any repairs or even painted the home in the five years she had lived there; she just didn't have the money. Joyce disclosed the work that needed to be done in the crawl space to the purchasers, and as expected, the purchase price was reduced. Joyce gave up home ownership and went back to renting, so someone else was responsible for repairs and upkeep.

This story not only conveys how important an emergency reserve is for expected unexpected repairs but also touches on something I haven't discussed yet.

When you are purchasing a home, the question is not whether you have enough money to pay the mortgage, homeowner's insurance, and property taxes but whether you have an additional amount either in your emergency reserve account or included in your spending plan to cover the expected expenses that accompany home ownership. This additional amount should be at least 4 percent of the purchase price of the home. Since Joyce paid $300,000 for her home, she needed a minimum of $12,000 per year for repairs and upkeep. This would either be in her spending plan at $1,000 per month ($12,000 per year) or in an emergency reserve account. If the latter, this amount is in addition to the reserve amount for three to six months of nondiscretionary bills. Since Joyce did not have this amount built into her spending plan or set aside in a reserve account, she would have been wise to purchase a less expensive home or continue to rent until she had saved this amount.

It is not an easy task to accumulate the amount needed to fund an emergency reserve account, so the best place to start, after you determine the amount of three to six months of nondiscretionary bills for you and your family, is to start putting at least 10 percent of your gross income into this account. Don't forget: this can only be done when you have your spending plan in place. Hopefully, your goal is to spend only 50 percent of your gross income. Opening a separate savings account or money market account is a good place to accumulate and keep your emergency reserve account.

The second type of reserve or savings account you will want to eventually set up is used for expected or planned large expenditures, such as college, vacations, a down payment for a home, cars, appliances, and so on. This account can be established once your emergency reserve account is funded.

Remember, the ultimate goal is to have the miraculous Rule of 72 working for you. Therefore, the sooner you meet the goals you have set in this chapter and the preceding chapters, the sooner you can invest part of your hard-earned paycheck into an investment account, which I will discuss in the next chapter.

Before moving forward, I would like to point out that there is one exception to funding your emergency reserve account with 10 percent of your gross income before you begin to invest. If your employer offers to match your contributions in their 401(k) plan, you will want to consider investing an amount equal to what they are willing to match (usually 2 to 4 percent) and put the remaining amount (6 or 8 percent) toward building your emergency reserve, instead of the entire 10 percent. If someone is willing to give you tax-free money, I suggest you say yes!

Suggested Goals

1. Determine the amount you need to fully fund your emergency reserve account.

   Determine the monthly amount you spend for your have-to-pay bills:

   i.   Mortgage/rent_____
   ii.   Utilities_____
   iii. Insurance_____
   iv.   Credit card minimums_____
   v.   Car payment(s)_____
   vi.   Other debt payments_____
   vii. Groceries _____
   viii. Other_____

   Total _____ × 3 if you are married and both spouses work

   Total _____ × 6 if you are single or married and only one spouse works

2. Go to your bank to open a separate savings account or money market account to begin accumulating your emergency reserve account for the expected unexpected expenses.

3. When your emergency reserve is fully funded with three to six months' worth of nondiscretionary expenses as well as your annual repair and maintenance reserve for your home (unless you are adding this amount to your spending plan), open another reserve or savings account or money market account to accumulate funds to use for expected, planned large purchases or large repairs.

If you are not able to begin funding your emergency reserve account, don't be stressed. These are steps and goals you want to act on when it is reasonable for your situation. Recall that you now have new understanding, which will provide you with new thinking and new goals. This is a journey, not something that will be accomplished today. For some, this journey will take a year to put in place, and for others, it will take three to five years. It could take even longer for others. It is not a race; it is a plan. If an individual fails to plan, he or she plans to fail. By having a plan, you are well on your way!

Ship your grain across the sea; after many days you may receive a return. Invest in seven ventures, yes, in eight; you do not know what disaster may come upon the land.

—Ecclesiastes 11:1–2 NIV

CHAPTER 7
INVESTING

I<small>F YOUR DEBT-MANAGEMENT RATIOS ARE IN LINE WITH THE</small> guidelines discussed in chapter 4, you have an emergency reserve established, and you are giving and living within your spending plan, then you are ready to have your money work for you by putting the Rule of 72 in motion. Many people are afraid to invest in the stock market, but this is simply because they do not understand it.

There are two concepts you will need to understand before investing. Gaining this understanding will change your thinking, and changing your thinking will help you develop the critical goals you need to obtain financial freedom. Financial freedom will assure you that your purse is full and no longer has any holes.

The first concept you should understand is that investing is for the long term. For example, if you are going to need the money in five years or less for a down payment on a home or for a new car, do not invest this money. Save the money in a savings account or money market account for expected planned purchases; do not invest it.

Investing is only for money that you are able to put away for long periods of time. It is to be used to build your financial freedom or your retirement. In order for the Rule of 72 to work, you must leave your money in the stock market, regardless of the ups and downs. The market will go up, and it will go down; that is just a fact. Over the long term, though, investing in the market is a positive experience. History shows us that if you had been invested in the market for the last thirty years, you would have earned an 8 percent return.

Carla had been investing for twenty years; the Rule of 72 was working for her. But in 2008, during the great recession, she let fear dictate her investment strategy. She sold all her securities, against the advice of her investment adviser and even her friends. She would not listen; fear had gripped her, and she cashed out. She felt she would be able to put the money back into the stock market later and not miss a beat. Unfortunately, this strategy, called market timing, can be devastating to an individual's investment portfolio. Studies show that those who cash out of their stock holdings during times of national disasters, geopolitical scares, epidemics, or economic gyrations and then try to pick the best time to come back into the market (supposedly on the upswing as the event dissipates) have significant losses that are almost impossible to recover.

Carla missed out on subsequent rebounds in the market, and it was a costly mistake. Research shows that had Carla stayed in the market the entire time during the twenty years beginning in 2002 and ending in 2021, she would have had an annual return of 9.5 percent.[5] However, because Carla pulled out of the market and missed the best five days in the market during those twenty years, her annual return was only 7.01 percent. If she had missed the ten best days during that same twenty-year time period, her annual return would have been only 5.31 percent. And if she had missed the forty best days in that time period, her annual return would have been -1.5 percent. Attempting to time the worst and best days in the stock market is impossible. Taking into consideration the Rule of 72, we know how important a higher rate of return is, and it is clear how much fear hurt Carla's investment portfolio.

Again, I want to reiterate this very important directive: only invest in the market for the long term; do not invest in the stock market in order to beat the market or time the market. This is gambling, and you have a greater opportunity to win in Vegas than you do in timing the market.

You can invest in other things, such as real estate, but for purposes of this book, I am focusing on the stock market. The stock market is favorable toward the Rule of 72 and the sooner this miracle starts working for you the better. In addition, many individuals reading this book will have the opportunity to invest in their 401(k) plans at work or set up their own IRA or Roth IRA, where stocks and bonds are

[5] Murray Coleman, "Market Timing: More Evidence Why It Doesn't Work," Index Fund Advisors, May 10, 2021, https://www.ifa.com/articles/market-timing_more_evidence_really_doesnt_work/.

used as the investment vehicles. Real estate is not normally used in these situations. Real estate may be appropriate for those who have the time and expertise in the area, but it is beyond the scope of this book.

The second concept to understand before you begin investing is asset allocation. Investments need to be properly allocated. Or, said a little differently, a stock portfolio needs to be diversified.

> Ship your grain across the sea; after many days you may receive a return. Invest in seven ventures, yes, in eight; you do not know what disaster may come upon the land. (Ecclesiastes 11:1–2 NIV)

Proper asset allocation accounts for 91.5 percent of the investment return in your 401(k) account, IRA, Roth IRA, or other type of investment account. This means you will want to divide the money you are investing into different categories of stocks and bonds.

If you are investing on your own rather than through an employer, find an investment person who is considered a fiduciary. Fiduciaries have a duty to invest in a way that benefits you, not themselves. An investment advisory representative (IAR) is a fiduciary who works for an investment advisory company, and I highly recommend utilizing someone with this designation. If an investment person says he or she is not a fiduciary, move on to the next person. Whomever you work with, an IAR or an adviser brought in by your employer for your 401(k), make sure he or she helps you determine your appropriate asset allocation. If your investment adviser does not want to diversify your investments, find an adviser who will. Ask others you respect whom they work with, or utilize the internet to search for an investment person who is an IAR. Once you find someone who is a fiduciary, perform a background check on him or her through the Securities and Exchange Commission (SEC) website. You want to make sure people are who they say they are. (See the "Suggested Goals" section at the end of this chapter for directions on how to conduct this search.)

Unfortunately, Diane and Frank did not perform a background check on their investment adviser. Their friend Connie, whom they respected very much, referred them to Barbara. Barbara was kind and warm, and Diane and Frank liked her. Because of their relationship with Connie, they decided to work with Barbara. Barbara earned their trust. Then, one day, Diane and Frank met with Barbara to review their investments and noticed their money was invested in accounts different from what they had originally agreed to. When Diane asked Barbara about this, Barbara said, "Oh, you signed a form that gave me discretionary authority to move your money wherever I felt was good for you."

Diane and Frank were horrified. They had not known they had given Barbara that kind of authority over their investments. If they had done a background check on Barbara, they would have seen eight customer complaints against her. They could have asked her about the complaints, and if Barbara's explanation had been unsatisfactory, they could have continued looking for an investment adviser who would consult with them regarding changes to their accounts and keep to the original plan they all agreed to. Barbara has since lost her licenses and is no longer managing money.

Asset allocations are different for each person and are based on age, goals, and the ability to handle risk. Each year, your allocation of stocks and bonds should be reviewed to determine whether your categories of stocks and bonds need to be rebalanced. Rebalancing means returning your asset allocation to its original allocation. This may be required due to several or all of your categories shifting (increasing or decreasing) because of market or other changes. If this sounds like a foreign language to you, go on the internet, and google *asset allocation*. There are dozens of sources via which you can learn more about this subject.

There are seven basic buckets, or categories, that make up your asset allocation. They include the following:

- Large-cap stocks
- Mid-cap stocks
- Small-cap stocks
- International stocks
- Mid-term bonds
- Short-term bonds
- Cash

A simple risk-assessment form given by your investment adviser or the adviser to your employer's 401(k) plan will help you allocate your investments in the most efficient and effective way for you. Just remember: diversification is key, and only invest money that you are able to keep invested for the long term.

One of the great things about investing in your employer's 401(k) account is that the amount of money you set aside from your paycheck to invest is not taxed in the year you invest it (up to $20,500 in 2022 and $27,000 if age fifty or older), nor is the resulting growth in the market. The Rule of 72 is working for you! The tax on the money you invest, as well as the growth, is deferred until you make withdrawals at retirement.

If you do not have an employer 401(k) plan available to you, you may be able to open up an IRA or Roth IRA. An IRA contribution is deductible (up to certain limits: $6,000 in 2022 and $7,000 if age fifty or older), and the earnings grow tax-free. As with the 401(k) plan, your contributions and market growth are not taxed until you make withdrawals at retirement. A note of caution: if you make withdrawals from an IRA or a 401(k) plan before age fifty-nine and a half, a 10 percent penalty could apply. There are exceptions for the penalty, but this is beyond the scope of our conversation. You can google the exceptions if you are contemplating withdrawing before age fifty-nine and a half.

A Roth IRA, on the other hand, is not deductible when you make the contribution. However, a Roth IRA permits you to withdraw your contributions tax-free after you have held the Roth IRA for five years. If you withdraw your earnings (market growth), you will be taxed on the amount of market growth withdrawn, unless you have held the Roth IRA for five years *and* have attained age fifty-nine and a half. Any withdrawal of market growth from a Roth

IRA before age fifty-nine and a half will also trigger the 10 percent penalty, just like an IRA or 401(k), even if you have had the Roth IRA account for more than five years.[6]

Additionally, an IRA requires that minimum required distributions (MRDs) be made by April 1 of the year after you reach age seventy-two. A Roth IRA does not have this requirement.

Investing is critical to financial freedom; it is, therefore, imperative you do not approach this subject with fear. There may be bad years, but proper asset allocation means you can handle the down years. Down years are normal. You are investing for the long term. As you give, stay within the debt-ratio guidelines, spend wisely, save for emergencies, save for planned purchases, and invest, you will be on your way to financial freedom and a full purse without holes. You are investing in yourself, and the attainment of your goals will have a great impact on your financial management and your joy. You will now have money working for you, and you can move on to fulfilling your God-given purpose and living a life you are passionate about.

---

[6] [6] Internal Revenue Service, "Distributions from Individual Retirement Arrangements (IRAs) for Use in Preparing 2021 Returns," Publication 590-B, https://www.irs.gov/publications/p590b.

Suggested Goals

1. I will commit to investing in myself by setting aside _____% of my gross income for investments and have the Rule of 72 work for me.

   Commit to one of the following:

   I will invest in my employer's 401(k) plan beginning _____.

   or

   I will open an IRA or Roth IRA with an investment person who is a fiduciary (investment advisory representative) beginning _____.

2. Do a background check on your existing investment manager or a potential investment manager by doing the following:

   1. Go to https://www.sec.gov.
   2. Click on the "Education" tab.
   3. Click on "Investor Education."
   4. Click on "Check Your Investment Professional."
   5. Enter the person's name, firm, and city and state if you have them. Click "Search."
   6. Click on "More Details." (This will let you know if the person is currently registered or is currently suspended. It will also tell you who his or her previous firms were, if any.)

7. Click on "Detailed Report." (This will provide you with even more information, which will help you corroborate what the adviser may have told you regarding licenses, education, and other business endeavors.)

8. If the person is suspended or has a troubled history, do not hire him or her.

3. You may perform an additional background check by doing the following:

   1. Go to https://www.finra.org/.
   2. Click on "BrokerCheck."
   3. Type in the person's name, firm, or CRD number (you can find the CRD number in the details on the SEC report above).
   4. Look for disclosures of any behaviors that are under investigation.

Rejoice always, pray continually, give thanks in all circumstances, for this is God's will for you in Christ Jesus.

—1 Thessalonians 5:16–18 NIV

CHAPTER 8
THANKFULNESS

A PASTOR FRIEND OF MINE, JACK, TAUGHT ME THAT thankfulness brings the miraculous. Being thankful for all you have been blessed with, even if you don't feel blessed, is the key to joy. Nothing can buy joy, but thankfulness will produce joy. Wouldn't it be great to walk around every day with joy in your heart? It can happen when you express continual thankfulness.

Even if something disastrous happens, find something to be thankful for in the midst of it; this will help keep you from falling into despair, depression, anger, hatred, or whatever emotion may be trying to take over. Just saying out loud that you are thankful for someone or something will make a big difference. You may have to say it more than once, and that's okay. Keep finding things to be thankful for until you feel peace, joy, or hope.

Personally, I have found that when I get upset with someone, if, instead of being angry or trying to figure out what happened, I say out loud that I am thankful for that person and his or her attributes, the anger disappears. It is miraculous! Or if I'm at a restaurant or a store and am not happy with the service, instead of fretting about it, I speak thankfulness that I can afford to go to the restaurant or the store or that I am able to be with the people who are with me. It makes an amazing difference in my attitude, peace, and joy.

> Rejoice always, pray continually, give thanks in all circumstances, for this is God's will for you in Christ Jesus. (1 Thessalonians 5:16–18 NIV)

Did you notice the above scripture says to give thanks in *all* circumstances? We don't only want to be thankful *for* things; we also want to be thankful *in* all circumstances. This means being thankful in delightful, joyful situations as well as difficult, gut-wrenching situations.

I experienced this vividly when I went through a difficult situation with a friend. My friend Madison hurt me deeply. I don't think she meant to, but she did. I was upset and sad. It took me a couple of days to even be able to pray about the situation. It then took several weeks to reconcile.

About three years later, the same thing happened. However, this time, I did not permit my emotions to take over, and instead of spiraling into depression and anger, I thanked the Lord for the situation. I thanked the Lord for

Madison and thanked him for the situation and for being my comfort and helper. I then asked for his wisdom in the situation and asked how I should handle the relationship. Wow! There was no anger, bitterness, or depression. I had joy in the situation—joy that the Lord gave me his wisdom on how to handle the situation and joy that I could pray for someone who had hurt me so much. Because I wasn't breathing venom and kept my joy, Madison ended up looking at herself and her attitude and came to me to ask for forgiveness. I was happy to forgive her and even happier that I'd learned how thankfulness could keep me above a situation instead of in the thick of it.

Take time to thank God, thank your spouse if you are married, thank your parents, thank your children, thank your friends, thank your pastor, thank your boss, thank your coworkers, thank a stranger, thank the waitress at lunch, or thank the bus driver. Develop the habit of being thankful, and you will change the direction of your life.

Thankfulness causes us to see just how blessed we are, which permits a stewardship mindset to permeate our thinking. This change in thinking is imperative if we desire a full purse with no holes. Let's move on and discuss the stewardship mindset.

Suggested Goal

Start and end your day with thankfulness. Think of at least five things you are thankful for each day.

God blessed them and said to them, "Be fruitful and increase in number."

—Genesis 1:28 NIV

Because you have been a faithful steward to manage a small sum, now I will put you in charge of much, much more. You will experience the delight of your master, who will say to you, "Enter into the joy of your Lord!"

—Matthew 25:21 TPT

For the one who has will be given more, until he overflows with abundance. And the one with hardly anything, even what little he has will be taken from him.

—Matthew 25:29 TPT

The righteous care about justice for the poor, but the wicked have no such concern.

—Proverbs 29: 7 NIV

CHAPTER 9
STEWARDSHIP OF THE PURSE

Before wrapping up this discussion of the journey to financial freedom and to having a purse that is part of the Purses Everywhere movement, I want to share how important stewardship is.

First, what is stewardship? Stewardship is being responsible for and taking care of all we have been given. We all have talents and skills that are unique to us. We were made to use these talents and skills to provide for ourselves as well as to enhance other people's lives.

As human beings and citizens of our country, we all have a responsibility to contribute and a responsibility to work. This may be in the home or outside the home. When we don't, something dies inside us, and an acute sense of worthlessness creeps in.

> God blessed them and said to them, "Be fruitful and increase in number."
> (Genesis 1:28 NIV)

We were made to be creative, to be prosperous, and to multiply. Our prosperity as a nation depends upon the personal financial prosperity of each one of us. Prosperity does not mean wealth; rather, it is defined as success. Success for us as individuals means we have accomplishments that are a direct result of utilizing our unique skills and talents. It means we are walking in our calling, which is exactly what we were made to do.

There are three different ways to think about financial freedom. Earlier, I shared that in order to have effective goals, we need correct thinking, and in order to have correct thinking, we need understanding. Therefore, it is important to understand the three different mindsets or ways of thinking about wealth and financial freedom.

The first mindset is one that focuses on scarcity, poverty, and fear. This mindset causes us to approach our finances with a glass-half-empty perspective.

The second mindset is the exact opposite of the first. It focuses on wealth at all costs, greed, unthankfulness, envy, and jealously. This mindset approaches finances with a wanting-all-the-glasses perspective.

Neither of these mindsets sounds particularly healthy, but there is a third mindset: the stewardship mindset.

This mindset says, "It is my responsibility to use the skills and talents I have been given to work. I prayerfully and responsibly spend. I am wise in my investing. I joyfully give to others. I'm thankful for all that I have." This is a glass-overflows perspective. In order to have a purse with no holes, we need the stewardship perspective, which thinks in terms of thankfulness instead of scarcity, fear, greed, and jealousy.

I hope by reading this book, you will begin thinking like a steward and have a stewardship mindset by being thankful and finding joy in giving. If you haven't already written down your goals, go back to each chapter, and write your goals. Don't forget to share your goals for financial freedom with a friend and follow through by sending a weekly progress report to your friend or group of friends. Also, I recommend praying with your friend about each other's goals. Remember the following verses:

> Because you have been a faithful steward to manage a small sum, now I will put you in charge of much, much more. You will experience the delight of your master, who will say to you, "Enter into the joy of your Lord!" (Matthew 25:21 TPT)

> For the one who has, will be given more, until he overflows with abundance. And the one with hardly anything, even what little he has will be taken from him.
> (Matthew 25:29 TPT)

I would like to add my commentary on the latter verse: if people are unfaithful with a little, what they have will be taken from them because of the holes in their purse.

Let me make one last comment about stewardship. Women are stewards of their families and children. This is an honor and a privilege. We are also stewards of the poor as well as stewards of women and children who are dealing with injustices. This includes economic injustice, such as poverty, which leads to other types of injustice, such as sex and human trafficking and sexual and physical abuse, just to name a few.

Pew Research shows that 61 percent of the world's population live on less than $300 a month.[7] As of January 2022, there are 7.9 billion people in the world. This means that more than 4.5 billion people live on less than $3,600 per year. Imagine—if you make more than $300 a month, you earn more than 61 percent of the world's population! Ten percent of this group live on less than sixty dollars per month. This latter group is considered to be below the international poverty line.[8]

When women join together, they can stop these injustices. Our sisters and children are being oppressed, tortured, raped, and murdered. Women are God's instruments of mercy and compassion. Let us bring forth the cry for justice.

---

[7] Rakesh Kochhar, "Are You in the Global Middle Class?" Pew Research Center, July 21, 2021, https://www.pewresearch.org/fact-tank/2021/07/21/are-you-in-the-global-middle-class-find-out-with-our-income-calculator/.

[8] Compassion International, https://www.compassion.com/poverty/poverty-around-the-world.htm.

I have always found it interesting that the symbol of justice in our country is a woman. The legacy left to us by the women who came before us is to give as well as to be advocates who stand for equal rights and justice for all. Let us move forward and focus on this heritage and our responsibilities as stewards of justice. Women carry compassion, mercy, and a desire for justice in their DNA. But in order to pull together to fight for economic justice in this country and world, we have to help ourselves and our families first.

> The righteous care about justice for the poor, but the wicked have no such concern. (Proverbs 29: 7 NIV)

I have written this book to help you put your financial house in order, no longer be subject to economic slavery because of holes in your purse, and remember we are stewards and holders of the purse for a reason. Instead of thinking only of ourselves, let's join together to bring poverty and slavery to an end. These injustices hurt us all.

Now is the time to stand up and do something. We cannot ignore our sisters' and children's cries for help any longer. There are many organizations doing their part; give these organizations what you can, whether it is your finances, time, or prayer.

Get involved with your church or community to help the poor and trafficked. Research organizations online, and commit to giving whatever you can. Eliminate the holes in your purse and let there be Purses Everywhere that open up and give.

I plan to give the profits from the sale of this book to organizations that help the poor or free women and children from trafficking. Think of what our world will look like when all 150 million women and girls in this country work together for economic justice and freedom from slavery in the United States and then all over the world! Let's not miss this opportunity; together we can do this.

May it be said of this generation of women who come together to free women and children caught in the bondage of trafficking and poverty and to fight economic injustice and give, "They were the generation that had purses everywhere."

Suggested Goals

1. Speak out loud to yourself the following affirmation daily:

   My cup overflows. I am a good steward, and I manage my finances well.

2. Send the goals you wrote at the end of each chapter to a friend, and be accountable to your friend. Pray with your friend about each other's goals.

3. Find a small way to help another woman or a child— perhaps supporting a woman-owned business or smiling at a child you see in the store who looks sad. Be intentional to do this daily.

Ask and it will be given to you; seek and you will find; knock and the door will be opened to you. For everyone who asks receives; the one who seeks finds; and to the one who knocks, the door will be opened.

—Matthew 7:7–8 NIV

AFTERWORD

I<small>F YOU HAVE NOT HAD THE BLESSED OPPORTUNITY TO RECEIVE</small> Jesus Christ as your Lord and Savior, all you have to do is ask.

Say, "Lord Jesus, I am a sinner, and I repent and ask forgiveness for my sins. I invite you to enter my heart, come into my life, and set me free from the bondage of sin."

It is that simple. Just listen, and you will hear him speak to you. This will do more for you than any financial gain, because it is for eternity; it is what we are created for, and we cannot do anything without Jesus.

> Ask and it will be given to you; seek and you will find; knock and the door will be opened to you. For everyone who asks receives; the one who seeks finds; and to the one who knocks, the door will be opened.
> (Matthew 7:7–8 NIV)

God bless you.

Suggested Goals

1. Tell someone what happened when you said the above prayer.
2. Buy a Bible, and read the Gospel of John.
3. Find a Bible-believing church to attend, and join a new believers' class.
4. Seek the Kingdom.

www.ingramcontent.com/pod-product-compliance
Lightning Source LLC
Chambersburg PA
CBHW021452210526
45463CB00002B/755